THE Dirty Girl's JOKE BOOK

THIS IS A CARLTON BOOK

First published in 2003 by
Carlton Books Limited
20 Mortimer Street
London W1T 3JW

Reprinted in 2008.

A CIP catalogue record for this book is
available from the British Library

ISBN 978 1 84732 197 8

editorial manager: **Judith More**
art director: **Penny Stock**
executive editor: **Lisa Dyer**
editor: **Lara Maiklem**
design: **DW Design**
cover design: **Zoë Dissell**
production controller: **Caroline Alberti**
illustrator: **Anna Hymas**

Printed and bound in England

THE Dirty Girl's JOKE BOOK

CARLTON
BOOKS

1

WHYS AND WHEREFORES

Why did God give women nipples?

To make suckers out of men!

What did Adam say to Eve when he got his first hard-on?

'Take cover! I don't know how big this thing gets!'

What does a Greek bride get on her wedding night that's long and hard?

A new surname.

What do you get when cross a lawyer with a blonde?

I don't know, but it sure enjoys screwing people.

What did the typhoon say to the coconut tree?

Hang onto your nuts this is going to be one hell of a blow-job.

What did the elephant say to the nude guy?

'It's cute, but can it pick up peanuts?'

What do you do when your husband turns 40?
Try to change him for two 20s.

What happened to the big-titted streaker at the pop concert?
She was thrown out by the bouncers.

Why do married men have strobe lights in their bedrooms?

To create the illusion they've managed to get their wives moving during sex.

Why do guys have a hole in their dick?

So oxygen can get to their brain!

Why do men like microwave dinners?

Because they like their food like their sex – finished in under five minutes.

Why do men like having sex with the lights on?

It makes it easier to put a name to the face.

How can you tell the characters in soap operas are fictional?

In real life, men aren't that affectionate out of bed.

Did you hear about the guy who had a penis transplant?

His hand rejected it.

How can you tell if a lesbian is butch?

She rolls her own tampons.

What's the best thing about being the oldest chick in a biker gang?

You don't have to pull up your tee-shirt so far when you're flashing your tits.

How do women get rid of unwanted pubic hair?

They spit it out.

How do you turn your sex toy into a snow plough?

Buy him a shovel.

What's pink, shrivelled and wrinkly and hangs out a man's trousers?

His mum.

What do a guy and a second hand car have in common?

They both have a tendency to misfire.

Why did the man cross the road?

He heard the chicken was a slut.

Why are men are like coffee?

The best ones are rich, warm and keep you up all night long.

Why are men like popcorn?

Because they fill a hole, but only for about five minutes.

Why are men like summer holidays?

Because they never seem to last long enough.

What does an elephant use for a tampon?

A sheep!

What's the square-root of 69?

Eight something.

What's the difference between a woman in a church and a woman in the bath?

One had a soul full of hope.

Why are men like cars?

They always pull out without checking to see if anyone else is coming.

What's the difference between tear-gas, a raw onion and a two-foot dick?

Nothing, they'll all make your eyes water!

What's the difference between purple and pink?

The grip.

What do men have in common with ceramic tiles?

Fix them properly once and you can walk all over them for life.

Why are women called 'birds'?

Because they tend to pick up worms.

Why can't gypsies have babies?

Because their husbands have crystal balls.

Question-master, to contestant: 'In the Garden of Eden, what were the first words Eve said to Adam?'

Contestant: 'Gosh, that's a hard one!'

Question-master: 'Well done. Two points.'

Five reasons why chocolate is better than sex

1 You don't get hairs in your mouth

2 If you bite the nuts, the chocolate doesn't mind

3 You don't need to fake enjoying it

4 It won't get you pregnant

5 It doesn't keep the neighbours awake!

2

GIRLS HAVE THE LAST LAUGH

An old sailor in a brothel is trying to make love with one of the girls. 'How am I doing?' he asks. 'Three knots,' says the girl. 'What d'you mean

three knots?' says the old geezer. The girl replies, 'I mean you're *not* hard. You're *not* in. And you're *not* getting your money back.'

A boss brings his secretary home after a dirty weekend. 'That was great,' he says. **'I bet you won't forget that in a hurry.'** The secretary replies, **'I could. What's it worth?'**

A man makes an obscene phone call to a girl. 'Hello, darling,' he gasps. 'If you can guess what's in my hand, I'll show you a good time.' 'No thanks,' says the girl. 'If you can hold it in one hand, I'm not interested.'

A woman is in bed with her husband's best friend. The phone rings, and the woman answers it. 'Okay,' she says. 'Yeah. That's fine. I'll see you later.' She turns to her lover and says, 'That was my husband.' **'Your husband!'** shouts the man. **'I've got to get out of here!' 'Don't worry,'** says the woman. **'He won't be home for hours – he says he's out playing cards with you.'**

A newly married couple have promised to be open and honest with each other, but the wife still won't tell her husband how many sex partners she's had. 'Look,' he says. 'Just tell me. I've told you how many people *I've* slept with. It's only fair.' 'Well, okay then,' says his wife. 'Now let me think. There was one, two, three, four, five, YOU, seven, eight, nine...'

A **male doctor** and a **female doctor** meet up at a medical convention. One thing leads to another and they end up in bed. Just before they get started, the woman dashes into the bathroom to wash her hands. After they've had sex, she gets up and washes her hands again. The guy says, 'Anyone who washes their hands that much **has to be a surgeon**.

'That's right,' say the woman. 'I am a surgeon. **And I bet you're an anaesthesiologist'**.

'Wow,' says the guy. **'You're right. But how did you guess?'**

The woman replies, **'Because I didn't feel a damn thing.'**

A soldier is stationed on a remote tropical island. To keep his mind off the beautiful native women, his wife sends him a harmonica and suggests the soldier learns how to play it. The solider writes back and says that he'll practice every night and won't even think of looking at another woman. Six months later the soldier returns home. He dashes upstairs and finds his wife waiting for him, naked in bed. He tears off his clothes and prepares to leap on her. 'Darlin',' he says. 'I sure have been looking forward to this!' 'So have I,' says his wife. 'But before we get started, will you do me favour?' 'Sure,' says the soldier. 'What d'you want me to do?' His wife throws a harmonica on the bed and says, 'Play me a tune.'

A travelling salesman books into a hotel and asks the clerk for a single room. As the desk clerk fills out the paperwork, the man sees a gorgeous blonde sitting in the lobby. She looks at him and gives him the come-on. They man goes over to make her acquaintance, then, after quick chat, he comes back to the reception desk with the girl on his arm. 'Fancy that,' he says to the clerk. 'I just met my wife here. I guess we'll be needing a double room for the night.' The next morning, the salesman comes down to settle his bill and finds he owes over £4,000. 'How can it be this much?' he yells. 'I've only been here for one night!' 'Yeah,' says the clerk, 'But your wife was here for two weeks.'

A **girl is on a train** and a **dirty old man** sits opposite her. The old git gets a bag of prawns out of his pocket and starts eating them, throwing the shells on the floor round the girl's feet. When he's finished, he screws up the bag and throws it at the girl's head. The girl picks up the bag, collects all the pieces of shell and puts them in the bin. Then she **pulls the emergency stop**. 'You silly cow,' says the old man. **'You'll get a £50 fine.'** The girl replies, **'Perhaps, but when the police smell your fingers you'll get five years.'**

A couple have **four daughters**. The three oldest are tall with blonde hair, while the youngest, Debbie, is short and dark. One day the **husband** is run over by a truck and his wife comforts him as they wait for the ambulance. The husband doesn't think he'll make it – he turns to his wife and says, 'Darling, I can't hang on for much longer. Before I die, answer one question – **is Debbie my daughter?** I always wondered.' 'Yes,' replies his wife. **'Of course she's your daughter. I swear it.'** Hearing this, the husband passes away peacefully. **'Phew!'** says his wife. **'Thank Christ he didn't ask about the other three!'**

A man walks into his local pub. One of his mates comes up to him and says, 'You put on a **great show with your girlfriend last night**. You left the light on in your bedroom – we could see everything you two got up to **projected on the curtains!** What a show!' 'Afraid not,' says the man. **'I wasn't even home last night.'**

A man comes home and finds his wife shagging the postman. **'Gladys!' he shouts. 'What are you doing!?' Gladys turns to the postman and says,** 'See. I told you he doesn't know the first thing about sex!'

A hooker tries to pick up a Salvation Army bandsman. **'Miss,' he says. 'Are you familiar with the concept of original sin?'** 'That depends,' says the hooker. 'But if it's really original, it'll cost you an extra £30.'

In the beginning, **God creates Eve and gives her three breasts.** Eve likes living in the Garden of Eden, but **she finds her middle boob a real pain.** It pushes the other two out and they keep getting in the way of her arms. **She complains to God** and he fixes the problem. He removes the middle boob and **throws it into a bush.** Some time later God comes back to check on Eve again. Eve is fine but she's lonely and wants a mate. 'You're right, Eve,' says God. **'I should have thought of that. I'll create you a mate called 'Man'. Now, all I need is something to work with. Let's see...Where did I put that useless tit?'**

A flat-chested girl goes out **shopping** for a **bra**. She wants a bra in **size 28A**, but can't find one anywhere. Eventually she comes across a little clothes shop run by an old deaf woman. 'Have you got anything in size 28A?' asks the girl. **'What did you say, dear?'** says the old woman, cupping her hand to her ear. The girl lifts up her tee-shirt and shows the old woman her boobs. 'Have you got anything for these?' she says. The old woman peers at the girl's chest and says, **'No. Sorry, dear. Have you tried Clearasil?'**

A secretary **is helping her new boss set up his** computer. **She asks him what word he'd like to use as a password. Being** a bit of a dick-head, he tells her to use the word 'penis'. **She looks at him and says,** 'Sorry. Not long enough.'

Two lap dancers are getting ready for a performance when one notices that the other isn't wearing her engagement ring. **'What happened to the ring?'** she asks. **'Is the wedding off?' 'Yeah,'** says the other. **'Yesterday I saw him naked for the first time – he looked really ugly without his wallet.'**

A husband says to his wife, **'I'm getting our phone number changed. Every day this week someone has rung us thinking we're the coastguard.' 'The coastguard?'** says the wife. **'Yes,'** says the husband. **'Some moron keeps calling to ask if the coast is clear!'**

A man comes **home unexpectedly** and finds his **oldest friend having sex with his wife. 'You asshole!'** he shouts. **'I've known you since I was ten years old. We went to school together. We were in the army. I saved your life. You were the best man at my wedding...Hey! Stop doing that while I'm talking to you...!'**

A man goes to a **massage parlour** and pays for a half hour session. As the masseur rubs the man's chest she notices he's developed a **huge erection**. She leans over and whispers, **'Would you like a wank?' 'Yes, please,'** replies the man. The girl slips out of the room and the man waits in anticipation. A minute later she sticks her head round the door and says, **'Have you finished?'**

An Italian girl is going on her first date. Her **mother warns her about boys.** 'They're only after one thing,' she says. 'Don't let him take liberties. **Don't let him feel your chest or your legs. Don't play with his privates, and don't ever let him get on top of you** – if you do that you will **disgrace your family**.' When the girl returns, her mother asks her how it went. 'We got soaked in the rain,' says the girl. 'So we had to go to his house and take our clothes off to dry them.' 'Mamma mia!' says mother. 'It's okay,' says the girl. **'I didn't let him feel my chest or my legs. And I didn't play with his thingy.** But when I said I wouldn't, he started playing with it himself and then he said we ought to lie down.' 'Mamma mia!' says mother. 'Don't tell me you let him get on top of you and disgrace your family. 'Oh no,' says the girl. **'I remembered what you said, so I got on top of him and disgraced HIS family.'**

A husband and wife are arguing. The husband shouts, 'When you die, I'm getting a headstone that says, **"Here lies my wife – cold as ever."**'
'Oh yeah?' she replies. 'Well, when you die, yours will read, **"Here lies my husband – stiff at last!"**'

A man comes home and finds his wife in bed with another man. He takes out a gun and shoots him. His wife says, 'Look. If you keep doing that you're not going to have *any* friends left at all!'

3

BOYS BEHAVING LIKE BOYS

The ten things men know about women:

1. ——

2. ——

3. ——

4. ——

5. ——

6. ——

7. ——

8. ——

9. ——

10. THEY HAVE BOOBS!

A man sunbathes in the nude and ends up scorching his dick. He goes to his doctor who advises him to bathe it in cold milk. That evening his wife comes home and finds him standing by the kitchen table with his lobster-red dick stuck in a glass of milk. 'Oh, right,' she says. **'I always wondered how you re-loaded those things.'**

A platoon of Marines is having a medical inspection. Their sergeant tells them to strip off and line up three rows outside the medical hut. The sergeant sees a man in the back row scratching his arm. He hits the man's elbow with a stick.

'Did that hurt?!' shouts the sergeant. 'No, sir!' replies the soldier. 'Why not?!' shouts the sergeant. 'Because I'm a Marine, sir!' yells back the soldier.

The sergeant then sees a man in the middle row rubbing his nose. The sergeant hits the man on the head. 'Did that hurt?!' yells the sergeant. 'No, sir!' is the reply. 'Why not?!' shouts the sergeant. 'Because I'm a Marine, sir!' yells back the soldier. The sergeant then sees a man in the front row with a huge erect dick sticking out between his legs.

The sergeant whacks the end of the erection with his stick and yells, 'Did that hurt soldier?!' 'No, sir!' replies the soldier. 'Why not?!' shouts the sergeant. The soldier says, 'Because it belongs to the man behind me, sir!'

On his retirement, a Jewish doctor who specialises in circumcision takes **all the foreskins he's saved** over the years and sends them to a luggage-maker. He wants all the foreskins turned **into a bag** as a retirement present to himself. A week later the doctor returns and the luggage-maker **gives him a wallet.** 'I gave you all those foreskins and you made me a wallet?' exclaims the surgeon. 'I wanted a bag at the least.' **'It is a bag,'** says the luggage-maker. **'If you stroke it, it turns into a briefcase.'**

A Texan goes into a tailor's to get measured for a suit. 'What's your waist size?' asks the tailor. '40 inches,' replies the Texan. 'We grow them big in Texas.' 'What's your outside leg?' asks the tailor. '54 inches,' replies the Texan. 'We grow them big in Texas.' 'How much space do you need in the crotch?' asks the tailor. 'I'm a three-incher,' replies the Texan. 'Three inches?' laughs the tailor. 'I'm four inches and I'm from California.' 'Hold on, sonny,' replies the Texan. 'We measure it different where I come from – that's three inches from the ground.'

A woman takes her **two dachshunds**, a male and a female, to the vet for a check-up. 'Has the male been neutered?' asks the vet. 'There's no need,' replies the woman. 'At home I keep the female upstairs and the male downstairs.' **'Can't the male climb the stairs?'** asks the vet. 'No,' replies the woman. **'Not when he's got a hard-on.'**

After spending years in the closet, Luigi decides it's time to **come out to his Italian mamma.** He finds her in the kitchen and tells her he's gay. Mamma is shocked. 'Luigi!' she says. 'You mean you don't like girls?' 'No mamma,' says Luigi. 'You mean you do all those dirty sex things with other men?' says mamma. 'Yes, mamma,' says Luigi. 'You mean you even put other men's dicks in your mouth?' asks mamma. 'I do, mamma,' says Luigi. 'I understand,' says mamma. She sighs deeply, then picks up a wooden spoon and starts whacking Luigi over the head with it, **'So you put men's dicks in your mouth, and you still have the nerve to complain about the taste of my lasagne...?!'**

What's a man's idea of foreplay?

Brushing his teeth.

Two guys are changing in a locker room. The first guy shows off his huge dick. 'It's a beauty isn't it,' he says. 'It's a transplant job. It cost me £15,000.' A few months later, the same two guys meet up again in the locker room. The second guy drops his pants and shows off *his* new dick. 'They cheated you when they sold you your transplant,' says the second guy. 'I had this one fitted last month and it only cost me £1,000.' The first guy peers at the other's dick and says, 'No wonder it was so cheap – that's my old one!'

Johnny's mum asks his dad to tell him about the birds and the bees. Dad sits Johnny down in front of the telly and puts on a hardcore porn DVD. After a few minutes, Dad points to the screen and says, 'You see all that? Birds and bees do that as well.'

John has his wife's name, Wendy, tattooed on his dick, but normally, he can see only the first and last letters, 'W' and 'Y' – he sees the whole name only when he has an erection. One year, John and Wendy go on holiday to Jamaica. They go on a minibus tour of the coast and stop off at lunch time for a rest-stop. John goes to take a piss and finds himself standing next to the minibus driver. John looks down and sees that the driver also has the letters 'W' and 'Y' tattooed on his dick. 'Excuse me,' says John, 'but I couldn't help noticing your tattoo – does it say "Wendy" like mine?' 'No,' says the driver. 'I work for the Tourist board. My tattoo says,

"Welcome to Jamaica, my friend, have a nice day."'

A cucumber, a pickle and a **penis** are moaning to each other. The pickle says, **'My life is terrible. When I get big, fat and juicy they're going to stick me in a jar full of vinegar.'** The cucumber says, **'Yeah? Well when I get big, fat and juicy, they're going to slice me up and toss me in a salad.'** The penis says, **'You think that's tough? Whenever I get big, fat and juicy, they put a bag over my head, shove me in a wet, dark, smelly room and make me to do pushups until I puke!'**

What do you call a man who's just had sex?

Anything you like – he's fast asleep.

A fireman tells his wife about the new system they have at work. 'Bell one rings and we all put on our jackets,' he says. 'Bell two rings and we slide down the pole, and when bell three rings we're on the fire truck ready to go.' 'So why are you telling me all this?' asks his wife. Her husband replies, 'Well, from now on, when I come home and say 'Bell one', I want you to take your clothes off. When I say 'Bell two', I want you to jump into bed. And when I say 'Bell three', we're going to screw all night.' So the next night the fireman comes home and yells, 'Bell one!' His wife promptly strips off. Then he shouts, 'Bell two!' And his wife jumps into bed. Then he yells, 'Bell three!', and they begin having sex. Suddenly his wife yells, **'Bell four!'** 'What the hell is Bell four?' asks her husband. **'Roll out more hose!'** she shouts. **'You're nowhere near the fire!'**

An American, an Australian and a German are bragging about **how long their dicks** are. To see who has the biggest, they go to the **top of a 15-storey building** and flop their tackle over the side. The German goes first and his dick dangles down to the tenth floor. The Australian goes next, and his flops down to the fifth floor. The American goes last, but as soon as his dick has gone over the side he starts dancing around and jerking his hips about. **'What are you doing?'** asks the German. The American replies, **'I'm dodging traffic!'**

Which is easier to make, a snowman or a snow-woman?

A snow-woman! With a snowman you have to hollow out his head and make the extra snow into a pair of testicles.

A man goes to a doctor and asks him to take a look at his dick. 'But promise you won't laugh,' says the man. 'I'm very sensitive about my penis.' The doctor agrees, but when the man drops his pants the doctor can't help laughing – the dick is miniscule. 'I'm sorry,' he says. 'But that's the smallest penis I've ever seen. It's so tiny, I can barely see it. So what seems to be the matter with it?' The man replies, 'It's swollen.'

What do you do with a guy who thinks he's God's gift to women?

Exchange him.

What's the toughest part of a man's body?

His dick. Because it can stand up to any cunt!

What do all men at singles bars have in common?

They're married.

What's the worst part of a man's body?

His dick – it has a head with no brains, hangs out with two nuts, and has an asshole as a next-door neighbour.

Why did early men learn to walk upright?

To leave their hands free for wanking.

A man goes to a brothel and says to the Madam, **'What can I get for five quid?'** 'Five quid!' says the Madam. **'You can piss off and have a wank.'** The man goes off. A few minutes later, he comes back and says, **'Who do I give the fiver to?'**

After a visit to a massage parlour, a man finds a painful lump on his dick. He goes to see a doctor. The doctor does a thorough examination, then says, 'I'm afraid this is serious. You know how boxers can get a cauliflower ear?' 'Yes,' says the man. The doctor replies, 'Well you've got a brothel sprout.'

A man wins a camel in a bet and rides it home. 'What the hell is that thing?' asks his wife. 'It's a male camel,' says her husband. 'How can you tell it's a male?' she asks. 'You don't know anything about camels.' 'It must be a male,' replies the man. 'On the way here at least ten people pointed at us and shouted **"Hey – look at the dick on that camel!"**'

A man is in the bedroom admiring his dick. He turns to his wife and says, 'You know what – two inches more, and I'd be king.' She looks at it and says, **'Two inches less, and you'd be queen.'**

4

CHAT-UPS AND COMEBACKS

Guy: 'I actually have a girlfriend, but tonight I gave her the evening off.'
Girl: 'What for – good behaviour?'

Guy: 'People think I'm a policeman because of the size of my love truncheon.'
Girl: 'Oh yeah, I remember Inch High Private Eye!'

Guy: 'Y'know, I could fulfill every sexual fantasy you have.'
Girl: 'Wow! You mean you have a donkey *and* a Great Dane?'

Guy: 'Are you the girl I was kissing at the party last night?'
Girl: 'I don't know. What time were you there?'

Guy: 'For the sake of the other women in this bar, I think we should leave together – you're making them all look ugly.'
Girl: 'I think we should stay – you're making all the other men look good.'

Guy: 'Hey, how about you and me going out for a drink?'
Girl: 'Sorry, I don't date outside my species.'

Guy: 'Excuse me, but didn't we go on a date once?'
Girl: 'It must have been once. I'd never make that mistake twice!'

Guy: 'Hey, beautiful. How did you get to be so good looking?'
Girl: 'I don't know – perhaps I got your share too!'

My friends said you're not fit to sleep with a pig. But I stuck up for you. I think you are.

Guy: 'Why do you bother wear a bra – you've got nothing to put in it.'
Girl: 'So? You wear underpants, don't you?'

Guy: 'I know how to please a woman.'
Girl: 'Great, I guess that means you're going to piss off.'

Guy: 'I want to give myself to you.'
Girl: 'Sorry, I don't accept cheap gifts.'

Guy: 'Can I call you. What's your number?'
Girl: 'It's in the phone book.'
Guy: 'But I don't know your name.'
Girl: 'That's okay. That's in the phone book too.'

Guy: 'I've got a 10-inch penis.'
Girl: 'I find that hard to swallow.'

Guy: 'Is this seat empty?'
Girl: 'Yes, and if you sit in it, so will mine.'

Guy: 'What radio station would you like me to switch on when I wake up in the morning?'
Girl: 'I don't know. What do they play at the hospital?'

I don't know what your problem is, but I bet it's hard to pronounce.

If I throw a stick, will you leave?

I'll bet your birth certificate is a letter of apology from the condom factory.

I'm blonde, what's your excuse?

You're obviously a man of many parts, it's a shame you're so badly assembled.

Why don't you pull your lip over your head and swallow!

Are you wearing a wig? I suppose you need it to cover the lobotomy scars.

Guy: 'You look like the kind of girl who's into S&M.'
Girl: 'I am. In fact I'm already visualising the duct tape over your mouth.'

Guy: 'You're one in a million.'
Girl: 'Yeah, and so are your chances.'

Guy: 'D'you want to come back to my place and have sex?'
Girl: 'Okay. But only if we do 68.'
Guy: 'What's 68?'
Girl: 'You go down on me and I'll owe you one.'

Guy: 'Has anyone told you you're the most beautiful girl in the room?'
Girl: 'Yes, and I didn't sleep with him either.'

Guy: 'Hi, can I buy you a drink?'
Girl: 'Sorry, I'm too busy right now. Can I ignore you some other time?'

Do you still love nature, despite what it did to you?

Some day you will find yourself – and wish you hadn't.

Do you often set aside this special time to humiliate yourself in public?

Oh, do you have to leave so soon? I was just about to piss in your beer.

Take off that stupid mask – Halloween's not for months!

Whatever kind of look you were aiming for, you missed!

Why don't you go and slip into something more comfortable, like a coma?

5

DIFFERENT SIDES OF THE FENCE

A couple visit a **sex counsellor** to see if they can improve their love life. 'Have you thought about **different positions**?' asks the counsellor. 'How about the Wheelbarrow? Your wife gets on her hands and knees, you stand behind her, lift up her legs, get inside her, and off you go!' When they get home the husband asks his wife if **she want to try the Wheelbarrow**. 'Well, okay,' she says. 'But on two conditions. First, if it hurts, you'll stop straight away. **And second, you have to promise we won't go past my mother's house.'**

Do you know that they've started giving Viagra to old men in nursing homes? **Apparently it keeps them from rolling out of bed!**

Two elderly widows are discussing their dead husbands. 'Did you have mutual orgasms?' asks one. 'No,' says the other. 'I think we were with the Prudential.'

A woman goes to her doctor and explains that her husband is **impotent**. The doctor writes her a prescription. 'This is strong stuff,' he says. 'Get this tonic and put **three drops** in his milk before he goes to bed. No more than that.' Two weeks later, the woman comes back. 'So how's you husband?' asks the doctor. 'He's dead,' sniffs the women. 'One night I put **thirty drops** in his milk by accident – I came back for an antidote so we can **shut the lid on his coffin**.'

After God had created Adam he noticed that he looked very lonely. He said 'Adam, I've decided to make you a woman. She'll love you, cook for you, clean for you, and be sweet to you.' Adam said, 'Fantastic! How much will she cost me?' God answered, 'An arm and a leg'. 'Well,' said Adam, 'in that case,

what can I get for a rib?'

A prospector goes to a **remote mining town** and is horrified to find that the locals use **sheep for sex** – they have to, there's not a woman for a hundred miles. The man resists temptation for as long as he can, but one night he

can't stand it any more. He goes out, finds a pretty young sheep in a field, and takes her home to bed. The next day, the man takes a walk into town with his new lady friend and visits the saloon. The man walks into the bar with the sheep, and the place goes silent – everyone stares at him in horror. 'What's the matter?' says the man. **'Don't pretend to be shocked. You all sleep with sheep too.'** 'Well, sure we do,' replies the barman. **'But never with the preacher's wife!'**

A woman goes into an adult shop to **buy a dildo**. The guy behind the counter shows her the best dildo they have – the Magic Dildo. 'The Magic Dildo will do whatever you want,' says the guy. 'Just say 'Magic Dildo my... something' it starts screwing you there.' Impressed, the woman buys one and leaves. While she's driving home the woman decides to try it out. **'Magic Dildo my shoulder!'** says the woman. The dildo jumps out of its box and it starts **buzzing over her shoulder and neck**. Then the woman says, **'Magic Dildo my pussy!'** and the dildo jumps under her skirt and **starts screwing her.**

Not surprisingly, the woman loses control of the car starts swerving over the road. A traffic policeman pulls her over. 'I'm so sorry, officer,' says the woman. 'It's this dildo I just bought. **It's a Magic Dildo and it took me by surprise.'** The policeman thought he'd heard every excuse there is, but this one has to be the craziest. 'Yeah, right,' he snorts. **'Magic dildo my ass!'**

A mother is cleaning her teenage daughter's room when she finds a bondage magazine hidden under her bed. She shows the magazine to her husband. 'What do you think we should do?' asks the woman. Her husband flicks through the magazine and says, 'Well, I don't think spanking her is going to help.'

A number of flights are cancelled due to bad weather and the airport hotel fills up. It gets so overcrowded that people have to share rooms, and three men find themselves sleeping in the same bed. The next morning the man on the right-hand side of the bed says, 'I had a great dream. I dreamt that a beautiful woman was wanking me off all night.' **'That's a coincidence,' says the man on the left-hand side of the bed, 'I had exactly the same dream – someone was giving me a hand job all night long.'** 'What a couple of perverts,' says the man in the middle. 'I had a very nice dream **– all about skiing.'**

Father O'Leary is having a wank in the cathedral vestry when a tourist sees him and takes his picture. 'Oh my God!' says Father O'Leary. 'I'll be ruined. How much d'you want for that camera?' 'Six hundred pounds,' says the tourist. Father O'Leary nips over to the bank with the tourist, pays him the money, then takes the camera back to the vestry. Sister Sarah comes by. 'That's a very nice camera, Father,' she says. 'How much was it?' 'Six hundred pounds,' replies Father O'Leary. 'Christ!' exclaims the Sister. 'Someone must've seen you coming!'

Jumbo the elephant has no interest in sex and refuses to mate with any of the female elephants in the zoo. His keeper calls in an animal sex expert who suggests that the keeper arouses Jumbo by stroking his dick with a long wooden pole. A few weeks later the expert phones the zoo to see if Jumbo has started mating. 'No,' said the zookeeper.

'Stroking him with a stick did give him a hard-on, but now we can't get him away from the TV when the snooker comes on.'

Two firemen are having sex in a smoke-filled room. The fire chief bursts in and sees them. 'What the hell is going on?,' he shouts. One of the firemen looks up and says, **'Jones is suffering from smoke inhalation, sir!'** The chief says, 'Well why aren't you giving him **mouth-to-mouth** resuscitation?' 'I did, sir,' replies the fireman. **'How the hell d'you think all this got started?!'**

When you're on the beach, how can you recognize a guy who uses an inflatable sex doll?

He's the one who ignores the bikinis and stares at the beach balls!

A woman is crying on a park bench. An old man comes by and asks her what's the matter. 'My husband was caught having sex with one of his patients,' she sobs. 'He's been cheating on me and now it looks like he'll be struck off.' 'That's terrible, ' says the old man. 'But look on the bright side – news like that can't get any worse.' 'Oh yes it can,' sobs the women. 'He's a vet!'

A man joins the Foreign Legion and is posted to a **remote fort** in the desert. When he gets there, the sergeant explains that there are no women for miles and **the men rely on camels for sex**. That evening, a herd of camels is released onto the fort's parade ground and the men go wild, chasing them all over the place. The new recruit watches with disgust. The sergeant sees him and comes over. **'What are you waiting for?' he says 'Get stuck in.'** 'What's the hurry?' replies the new recruit. 'There must be over a hundred camels running around.' 'Well suit yourself,' says the sergeant. **'But don't blame me if you get stuck with an ugly one.'**

A man falls asleep on a beach and gets a really bad sunburn. His wife takes him to hospital and watches as a doctor covers him from head to foot in skin cream. Then the doctor gives the man some Viagra. 'Viagra?' says the wife. 'What good will Viagra do in his condition?' 'Not much,' says the doctor. **'But it'll help keep the sheets off him.'**

An old lady walks into a psychiatrist's office. 'Doctor,' she says. 'I think I might be a nymphomaniac.' 'I can help you,' replies the psychiatrist. 'But I'm expensive: I charge £100 an hour.' 'That's not bad,' replies the old lady. 'But how much for the whole night?'

A man goes into a public toilet and sees a man with no arms standing by the urinal. The armless man turns to him and says, 'Could you help me, please? My zip needs undoing.' 'Okay,' says the first man, and he pulls down the man's zip. The armless man then says, 'Could you take it out for me?' 'Um, well, okay,' says the first man. He pulls the armless man's dick out of his pants and sees that it's covered in **red bumps, green veins and brown scabs oozing with yellow goo. It really stinks too!** 'Could you point it for me?' asks the armless man. The other man tries to hold the horrible dick steady while the armless man has a pee. When he's finished, the armless man says, 'Now could you put it back in?' 'Sure,' says the first man. He shakes the putrid dick dry, stuffs it back in the armless man's trousers and does up his fly. 'Thank you,' says the armless man. 'I really appreciate that.' 'No problem,' says the first man. 'But I've got to ask you something – what the hell is wrong with your dick?' The other guy pulls his arms out of his jacket and says, **'Damned if I know, but I sure ain't touching it...'**

An old lady goes into a sex shop. She asks to see the dildos and the sales clerk shows her a display cabinet full of them. After having a good look, the old lady goes back to the counter. 'Could I have the 14-inch Ramrod in black,' she says. 'And the 24-inch double-ended one in pink, and the big red one on the wall.' 'Well I can get you the first two,' says the clerk. 'But the last one has to stay where it is – that's the fire extinguisher.'

A blonde goes to see her doctor. She has really bad constipation **and her doctor gives her a course of suppositories to cure it. After two weeks, the blonde still hasn't had a crap so she goes back to the doctor. 'I'm surprised,' says the doc. 'Those suppositories usually work like a charm. Have you been taking them regularly?' 'Of course, I have,' snaps the blonde.** 'What d'you think I've been doing – sticking them up my ass?'

A woman goes into a coma after a car crash. One day, a hospital doctor rings the woman's husband and tells him there's been a change in her condition – when the nurses wash her, they've noticed a response when they touch her breasts. The doctor suggests that the husband visits his wife and tries rubbing her breasts himself. The husband does so and there are definite signs of awareness. Next, the doctor suggests that the man massages his wife's privates. The husband does so and the response is even greater – it looks like she might be waking up! Finally the doctor suggests something even more stimulating – oral sex. The man goes into his wife's room, but a couple of minutes later her heart monitor starts beeping like crazy. The doctor runs in to help. 'My God!' he says. 'What happened?' 'I don't know,' replies her husband. 'I think she choked!'

A **female dwarf goes to a doctor** – her fanny is really sore and she has no idea why. The doctor tells her to lie down and lift up her skirt so he can examine her. A moment later he picks up a pair of scissors and starts snipping away at something. When he's finished he tells the dwarf to stand up, walk around, and see if she feels any better. 'That's much better,' says the dwarf. 'My fanny's not sore at all now. What did you do?' The doctor replies, **'I trimmed the top off your wellies.'**

A woman is about to have an operation. She's laid on a trolley and wheeled into the corridor. The nurse leaves her outside the operating theatre and goes to tell the surgeon she's ready. A man in a white coat comes by, lifts up the woman's sheet and peers at her naked body. He then calls over to another man in a white coat who comes over and has a look as well. 'Is something the matter?' asks the woman. 'I wouldn't know,' says the first man. **'We're just here to paint the ceiling.'**

6

TAKING PRECAUTIONS

A researcher asks a woman if she'd like to do some market research on condoms. 'It depends,' says the woman. 'What's in it for me?'

A woman is standing at a bus stop when it **starts to rain**. The man next to her is **smoking a cigarette** and as the first drops fall, he takes a **condom** out of his pocket, snips off the end, and **slips it over** his cigarette to **keep it dry**. The woman is a smoker too. She thinks this is a great idea and hurries over to a chemist's shop. 'Can I have a packet of condoms,' she says. 'Certainly, madam,' says the chemist. 'What size?' The woman replies, **'One that will fit a Camel.'**

A couple are relaxing after having sex. The woman says, 'If I got pregnant, what would we call the baby?' The man pulls off his condom, ties a knot in it, and flushes it down the toilet. 'Well,' he says. 'If he can get out of that, let's call him Houdini.'

Don't believe them when they tell you condoms are safe – a friend of mine was wearing one and he got hit by a bus.

Did you hear about the new 'morning after' pill for men?

It changes their DNA.

Have you heard about the new super-sensitive condoms?

After the man leaves they hang around and talk.

Wear camouflage condoms – they won't see you coming.

What's a married man's definition of safe sex?
Meeting his girlfriend at least 50 miles from his house.

A man goes into a chemist's to buy some condoms. He's confused by the shelves and shelves of condoms on display, and calls over a sales assistant to help. 'What size?' asks the sales assistant. 'I'm not sure,' replies the man. So the assistant sticks her hand down the guy's pants and has a feel. 'Medium,' she says and hands him a packet of condoms. A second man comes by and asks for help too. He doesn't know his size either so the assistant has a feel down his pants. 'Medium,' she says and hands him a packet of condoms. Next a schoolboy comes up to her. 'What do you want?' asks the assistant. 'Condoms,' says the boy. 'What size?' asks the assistant. 'Don't know,' says the boy. So the assistant puts her hand down his pants and has a rummage. Then she leans over to a microphone, presses the button and says, 'Clean-up in aisle five! Clean-up in aisle five!'

Mary and Patrick practise the **'stool and saucer'** method of contraception. Patrick (who is 5 feet 5 inches tall) and Mary (6 feet, 3 inches tall) make love upright, with Patrick standing on a stool and Mary leaning against a wall.

When his eyes get as big as saucers – she kicks away the stool.

7

THE GOOD, THE BAD AND THE UGLY

Good: Your boyfriend finally cleans out his bedroom.
Bad: You find a pile of old porno tapes in his bin.
Ugly: Your mother is starring in most of them!

Good: Your boyfriend gets on well with your parents.
Bad: He says he has more in common with your mum than you.
Ugly: He elopes with your dad!

Good: Your boyfriend is concerned about your health.
Bad: He tells you he might have given you the clap.
Ugly: He thinks he caught it off a goat!

Good: You can't find your vibrator anywhere.
Bad: You suspect your husband has been messing around with it.
Ugly: You hear a humming sound whenever he bends over!

Good: Your friend sets you up with a blind date.
Bad: He's short, bald and morbidly obese.
Ugly: He won't return your calls!

Good: The recruitment agency finds you a job.
Bad: They send you to a sleazy strip club.
Ugly: You're their new cleaning lady!

Good: You give the birds and bees speech to your 14-year-old daughter.
Bad: She keeps interrupting you.
Ugly: With corrections!

Good: Your boyfriend enjoys going clothes shopping with you.
Bad: You catch him wearing your new dress.
Ugly: He looks better in it than you do!

Good: Your boyfriend likes to keep the lights on while he's having sex.
Bad: He also likes to keep the curtains wide open.
Ugly: You first notice this while waiting at the bus stop opposite his house!

Good: Your boyfriend likes showing you off to his friends.
Bad: He secretly films you doing a striptease.
Ugly: It brings the house down on 'You've Been Framed'!

Good: Your boyfriend has an 18-inch tongue.
Bad: He has to be in the next room to go down on you.
Ugly: He keeps breaking off to catch flies!

8

SHAGGY TALES

A man goes to his doctor and says, 'I got this problem. **My wife always wakes me up at 1am for sex,** and then at 5 am so we can do it again before I go to work.' 'I see…' says the doctor. 'There's more,' says the man. 'When I get on the train I meet this girl every day. We get a compartment to ourselves and **screw all the way into town.** Then, when I get to the office I usually **give my secretary one** in the storeroom.' 'I see…' says the doctor. 'No. There's more,' says the man. 'When I go to lunch I always meet up with this waitress and we nip into a back alley **for a half-hour shag.'** 'Now I understand...' says the doctor. 'No. There's more,' says the man. 'When I get back to the office I have to spend the afternoon having **sex with my boss.** She says she'll give me the sack if I don't.' 'Ahh...' says the doctor. 'Now I see...' 'No. There's more,' says the man. 'When I get home, **my wife gives me a blowjob** before dinner, **another one afterwards** and then we have **sex till midnight.'** 'I see,' says the doctor. 'Have you finished now?' 'Yes,' says the man. **'So what exactly *is* your problem?'** asks the doctor. 'Well, y'see doc...' says the man. **'It hurts when I masturbate...'**

A woman goes to see her doctor. 'Every time my husband climaxes in bed, he lets out this ear-splitting yell,' she says. 'Well that's quite natural,' replies the doctor. 'What's the problem?' The woman replies, 'The problem is, it wakes me up.'

A doctor is having sex with one of his female patients. Suddenly her husband bursts into the room holding a shotgun. The doctor panics. 'It's not what it looks like!' he shouts. 'I was only taking her temperature!' 'Oh yeah?' says the husband aiming his gun at the doctor's crotch. 'Then you'd better hope it's got some numbers on it when you take it out!'

A little girl goes up to her mother and says, 'Mum, every night I hear you and Daddy making 'noises. And when I look in your room you're bouncing up and down on him.' Mother thinks quickly and says, 'I bounce on your Father's tummy like that because he's fat and it makes him thin again.' 'Well that's not going to work,' says the girl. 'Why not?' asks mum. The girl replies, 'Because the lady next door comes by every afternoon and blows him back up again!'

A little girl goes up to her dad and says, **'Daddy when my cat died, why did it lie on its back with its legs in the air?'** Daddy replies, **'Well its legs were up like that to make it easier for Jesus to grab him and pull him up to heaven.'** 'Wow,' says the girl. **'That means Mummy almost died this morning!'** 'What d'you mean?' asks Dad. The girl replies, 'After you'd gone to work, I looked into Mummy's room. **She was lying on the bed with her legs in the air shouting "Jesus! I'm coming!" and if it hadn't have been for the milkman holding her down, he would have got her!'**

A man takes early retirement and buys a remote cottage in the Scottish Highlands. One day, he hears a knock on the door and finds a huge, bearded Scottish farmer standing outside. 'I hear you're new here,' says the farmer. 'That's right,' replies the man. 'Then I'd like to invite you to a party I'm having,' says the farmer. 'Thank you,' says the man. 'I'd love to come.' 'I warn you though, there'll be lots of drinking,' says the farmer. 'I like a drink,' replies the man. 'And there might be a bit of rough stuff too,' says the farmer. 'That's okay,' says the man. 'I can take care of myself.' 'And things might get a bit frisky later on,' says the farmer. 'There'll be some hanky panky going on, no doubt.' 'That sounds great,' says the man. 'I like the ladies.' 'Och, there'll be no lassies,' says the farmer. **'It's just the two of us.'**

Teacher asks her class to say a sentence with the word 'beautiful' in it twice. Little Johnny stands up and says, 'My dad bought my mum a beautiful new dress and she looked beautiful in it.' 'Very good, Johnny,' says teacher. Then little Michael stands up and says, 'Yesterday was a beautiful day and I saw a beautiful flower.' 'Well done, Michael!' says teacher. She then turns to little Suzie and asks her if she can think of a sentence. Little Suzie thinks for a moment, then says, **'Last night my big sister told my dad she was pregnant, and he said, "Beautiful, fucking beautiful!"'**

Two Irish nuns are walking on the beach when they come across some secluded dunes and decide to do some sunbathing. **They both strip off and lie naked on the sand, soaking up the sunshine**. Suddenly one of the nuns realises they're being **spied on by a pervert with a camera.** The pervert is hiding behind a bush taking pictures of the naked nuns. However he's so worked up he's **not even looking through the viewfinder,** he's just snapping away at random. One of the nuns calls out, **'Hey! Aren't you going to focus?'** The other nun says, **'Give him a chance, sister. Let him take his pictures first.'**

Little Johnny has a brand new watch and little Suzie asks how he got it. **'Yesterday I got home early,'** says Johnny. **'And I heard noises coming from Mum and Dad's bedroom. I walked in and saw Dad and the lady from next-door bouncing in bed. Dad said I could have anything I wanted if I didn't tell mummy, so I asked for a watch.'** Suzie decides she'd like a watch too. That night she listens outside her parents' bedroom and hears some banging and groaning. **She walks in and finds her mummy sitting on daddy.** 'What do you want?' asks mummy. Suzie says, **'I want a watch.' 'Well, okay,'** sighs mummy. **'But stand in the corner and don't make any noise.'**

A Duchess is discussing Christmas presents with her maid. 'What present should I get the butler?' she asks. 'A bottle of wine?' suggests the maid. The Duchess frowns. 'He doesn't need that. I'll get him a tie. Now what about the cook?' The maid replies, 'What about some perfume?' The Duchess tuts, 'She doesn't need perfume. I'll get her an apron.' 'Now,' says the Duchess. 'What about my husband?' The maid says, 'I assume you want to get him something he really needs, madam?' 'Of course,' says the Duchess. The maid replies, 'Well in that case, how about five more inches?'

A husband comes home and finds his wife in bed with another man. **He drags the man into the garage puts the guy's dick in a vice and picks up a hacksaw.** The man screams, **'For God's sakes don't do it! Don't cut it off!'** The husband takes the handle off the vice, gives the man the hacksaw and says, **'I'm not going to cut it off. I'm going to set fire to the garage.'**

A couple are celebrating their silver wedding anniversary when the husband asks his wife if she's ever been unfaithful. **'Three times,'** answers the wife. 'Remember when you needed money to start your business? **Well I slept with the bank manager to get you a loan.'** 'So that's why he gave me the money,' says the astonished husband. His wife continues, 'The second time was when **I slept with the surgeon who did your heart operation.** He was the only one who specialised in your condition and we couldn't afford his fees.' 'Oh my God,' says the husband. 'You saved my life. And what was the third time?' 'Well,' says his wife. **'Remember when you wanted to be President of the Golf Club and you were 42 votes short...?'**

A guy goes into a pharmacy to buy condoms. The pharmacist says the condoms come in packs of 3, 9 or 12 and asks which one he wants. 'Well,' he said, "I've been seeing this girl for a while and I want the condoms because I think tonight's the night. We're having dinner with her parents, and I've got a feeling I'm going to get lucky after that. Once she's had me, she'll want me all the time, so I better have the 12 pack.' The guy buys the condoms and leaves. Later that evening, he sits down to dinner with his girlfriend and her parents. He asks if he might give the blessing and begins the prayer, but continues praying for several minutes. The girlfriend whispers to him, 'You never told me that you were so religious.' The guy whispers back,

'You never told me your father is a pharmacist.'

Little Suzie runs into class late. 'I'm sorry I'm late, miss,' she says, 'I had to make my own breakfast this morning.' Teacher doesn't believe this and makes Suzie answer some geography lessons as a punishment. 'Suzie,' says teacher, 'Point to this map and show me where the Scottish border is.' 'He's not on the map,' says Suzie. 'He's in bed with mum – that's why I had to make my own bloody breakfast!'

A guy goes to his girlfriend's house for dinner and his girlfriend tells him about an odd family custom – **the first person to speak after dinner has to wash the dishes.** The family sits down to eat and the dinner goes very well, but after it's over everyone sits around the table in silence. The guy doesn't want to wash the dishes so **he tries to create a commotion** by doing something outrageous. First he leans over and **sticks his hand down his girlfriend's blouse.** Everyone is silent, so the guy puts **his hands up his**

girlfriend's skirt. Still no one says a word. The guy pulls out all the stops. **He strips his girlfriend's clothes off and they bonk on the table.** Still no one speaks. The guy is not to be beaten. He tries again, but this time **he bends his girlfriend's mother over the table and has sex with her.** Still no one says a word. The guy gives up – these people must really hate washing up! **He sighs and starts to clear the table. He picks up the butter dish and the father jumps out of his chair. 'Okay, okay!'** he shouts. ***'I'll* do the damn dishes!'**

A man calls home one afternoon to talk to his wife. A little girl answers the phone. 'Hi, honey, it's daddy,' says the man. 'Is mummy there?' 'No, daddy,' says the girl. 'She's upstairs with Uncle Billy.' The man says, 'But you don't have an Uncle Billy.' 'Yes I do,' says the girl. 'He's upstairs in the bedroom with mummy.' 'Here's what I want you to do,' says the man. 'Put down the phone, knock on the bedroom door and tell mummy and Uncle Billy that daddy's car has just pulled up outside the house.' A couple of minutes later, the little girl comes back to the phone. 'I did what you said, daddy. When they heard me, mummy screamed, ran to get dressed, then tripped on the rug and broke her neck.' **'Oh my God!' says the man.** 'Then Uncle Billy jumped out the window into the swimming pool,' continues the girl. 'But he must have forgot that you took out all the water last week, because he broke his neck too.' There's a pause, then the man says, 'Swimming pool? Is this 443 8876?'

The headmistress of a girls' school asks the local vicar to give her pupils a talk about religion and sex. The vicar agrees, but his wife is very straight-laced so he tells her he's going to give the girls a talk about sailing. Next week, the headmistress meets the vicar's wife in the supermarket and tells her what a great talk her husband gave. 'It can't have been that good,' says the wife. 'He's only ever done it twice – the first time he was sick, and the second time his hat blew off.'

A doctor is doing the rounds of a maternity ward. He turns to the nurse and says, 'And when is Mrs Brown's baby due?' 'The 5th of October' replies the nurse. 'And how about Mrs Wise?' asks the doctor 'She's due on the 5th too,' replies the nurse. 'And Mrs Mills?' asks the doctor. 'Her baby is also due on the 5th,' replies the nurse. 'Don't tell me,' says the doctor. 'I'll bet that Mrs Carter's baby is due on the 5th as well.' 'No,' replies the nurse. **'Mrs Carter didn't go on the church picnic.'**

An Aussie rancher comes across a remote farmhouse and finds a girl sitting on the porch. **'D'yer screw?'** he asks. **'Not usually,'** she replies. **'But ya talked me into it ya smooth-tongued bastard.'**

Teacher walks into her classroom on Monday and sees that someone had **written 'dick' on the blackboard.** She gives her class a stern look then rubs the word off the board. The same thing happens the next day, except that this time **'dick' is written in much larger letters.** Again, teacher gives her class a glare and rubs the word off the board. Unfortunately, this goes on all week, and **each day the word 'dick' gets bigger and bigger.** Finally teacher comes into class on Friday and finds 'dick' written in huge letters right across the blackboard. **Underneath is a note saying, 'Dick. The more you rub it the bigger it gets!'**

A blonde, a brunette and a redhead are locked in a cell. The redhead takes out a mouth organ and says, 'At least I can play some music and pass the time.' The brunette pulls out a pack of cards and says, 'We can play games too.' The blonde pulls out a packet of tampons and says, 'And these are going to be great fun!' 'What do you mean?' asks the redhead. 'Those don't look fun to me.' 'Of course they are,' says the blonde. 'On the packet it says we can use them to swim, play tennis and ski.'

A girl brings her boyfriend home after a night out. The boyfriend is **desperate to use the toilet** but the girl is afraid he'll wake her parents if he goes upstairs. **'Go and use the kitchen sink,'** she whispers. **'No-one will know if we rinse it out later.'** So the boyfriend nips into the kitchen. A few minutes later he sticks his head round the door. **'Have you finished?'** asks the girl. **'Not quite,'** says the boyfriend. **'Have you got any paper?'**

Teacher asks her class to talk about a something they think is important. Little Suzie volunteers and walks to the front of the class where she draws a tiny dot on the blackboard. 'What's that?' asks teacher. **'It's a period,'** replies Suzie. 'Well it's very nice,' says teacher. 'But is it important?' 'I guess it must be,' says Suzie. **'This morning my big sister said she'd missed hers, and daddy had a stroke, Mummy passed out, and the man next door shot himself.'**